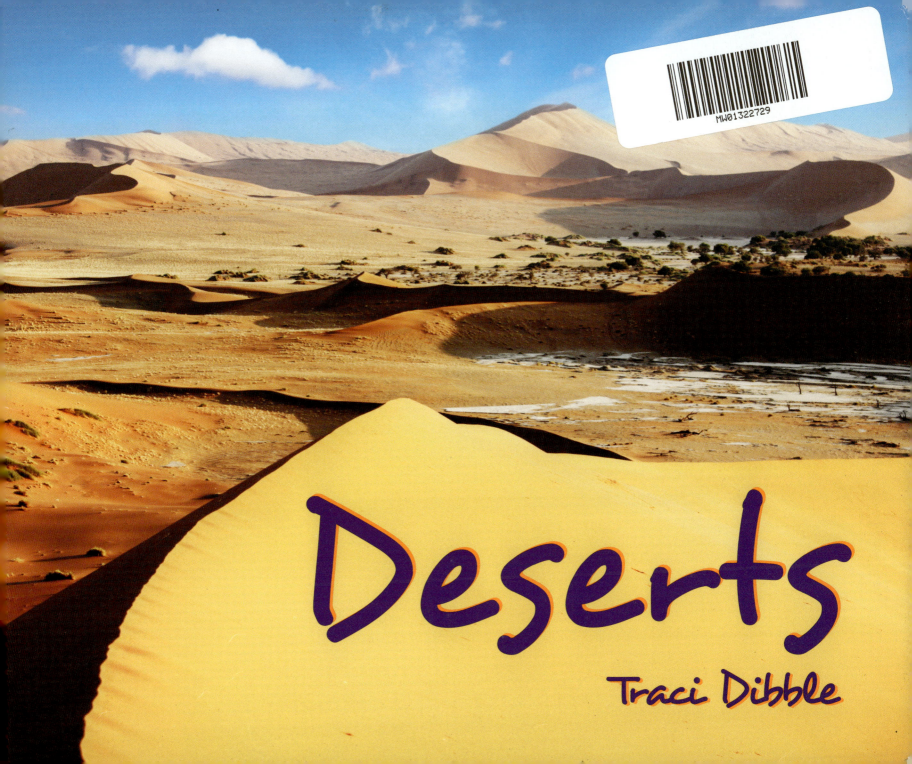

Deserts

Traci Dibble

Deserts can have sand.

Deserts can have rocks.

Deserts can have mountains.

Deserts can have snow.

Deserts can have lightning.

Deserts can have water.

Deserts can have grass.

Deserts can have flowers.

Deserts can have trees.

Deserts can have cacti.

Deserts can have beetles.

Deserts can have spiders.

Deserts can have lizards.

Deserts can have snakes.

Deserts can have rabbits.

Deserts can have camels.

Deserts can have birds.

Deserts can have lions.

Power Words

can
have